Brilliant

GW01458153

Locke A

BookLeaf
Publishing

Presentation by *BookLeaf Publishing*

Web: www.bookleafpub.com

E-mail: info@bookleafpub.com

ISBN: 978-93-95890-84-7

First edition 2022

DEDICATION

For everyone who ever felt the world collapsing
on them, and couldn't put it into words.

ACKNOWLEDGEMENT

Thanks to Ashley Walker, Ashuri472, for the wonderful cover art. Thank you to Bookleaf Publishing for the chance to be heard.

Intrinsic

The main character can sleep no more
For the ashes grew cold beneath
The wounded body
And the living can wait no longer
Wishing to encase the day
Before the fire runs out

Daydream

Noticing the limbs you use unconsciously
The chest used to live
The mind full of chaos
Every pain a malignant anomaly
Yet the only paradox
is the unrecognizable entity in the mirror

The stranger hosting your soul

Entirety

To the secrets behind your eyes
The skeletons in your closet
I believe in your facade
I will befriend your honest lies.

Halt

My breath repeats
Yours has ceased
My body aches and weeps
And yours, forever sleeps

Imbalance

My passion for downfall in exchange for my
hatred of trust
Sabotage the enjoyment of life against my will
I am the opposite of my opposite.

Restoration

The basic need for survival prevents the mind
from continuing
If I could swallow my pride, how many calories
is that?

Red

As it piles up weighing on your heart but
flooding through your mind,
Resolutions that make little sense, will in this
moment.
This moment you forgive in memory but not in
reality.

Home

Retreat, even if there's no peace to return to,
Its form physical but emotionally colder than
what it intends to be,
Only temporary, a resting place only heard
within.

Quotation

Cite the very expression and date it in the
present,
As evidence of where and when I expressed
myself

And wasn't lovable.

Frame

Capturing that I'm harder to break than I look,
but never acknowledging my transparency
My eyes are only windows to a sorrow
unspeakable
My body, evidence.

Press

Heartbeat that doesn't align with the tempo,
Eyes flicking back and forth, in and out of focus
The weight of abnormality showing in
uncontrollable gestures,
Gestures that bring you comfort,
While being disconnected in reality

Extend

Through this week,
This day,
The next event,
The next hour,
To the second my emotions decrease in volume,
I wait.

Paper

A mutual interest that divides
Weighing the rate and quality of life
To preach a moral high ground to stand above
the suffering
In order to sin and survive.

Vicariously

Envy for the unfortunate
Sadness for the wise
Wine for the young
Lies for the eyes.

Function

A vessel, a ghost
Combined to operate the machine.
One isn't acknowledged without the other
What can be described as malfunctions are
recognized when they're seen and not heard
What lives as a memory dependent on if marks
are left behind in the remains.

Radar

To locate the source of suffering is a larger landmark
Than the memory of now escaping into the past
Evaporating into smoke that grips without explanation
Forgotten. Remembered.

Stagnant

A limited time for a window of opportunity
Lost in comparisons
Drawing a shadow on the talent disappearing
into the many
Outshined and outdated.

Channel

To turn back and undo mistakes
Redo the positive
Is an emotion worth surviving for
Even if the wish will never come true
But remains a small possibility tomorrow.

Grip

I am no longer the memory of happiness,
To grow and change into a stranger
But mutually so
Selfishly desire to return to the time
When love was new

Glass

Guardian of betrayal
Endless apologies of empty value
The lies that transformed
Metamorphic heart
Under the pressure of adults

Rain

The comfort of the ambient world settles
The sore heart with ease
To blur the world out of focus
And bring a temporary peace.

9 789395 890847